I writ these songs in a dead man's book;
I stole the strain from a dead man's look;
And if much of death there may seem to be
'Tis because the dead are so dear to me.

All images are from the University of Dundee Archive Services

POEMS FROM THE GREAT WAR

Joseph Lee

First published in Great Britain in 2014 by

Discovery Press
University of Dundee, Dundee, DD1 4HN

ISBN: **9781 84586 2374**

British Library Cataloguing-in-publication Data
A catalogue record for this book is available on request from the British Library.

Typeset by **Chris Collins, Fife.**
Cover design by **Chris Hannah Design**.
Printed and Bound by **Bell & Bain, Ltd, Glasgow**.

DEDICATED
TO HIM :—

Contents

Sergt
The Black Watch
Belgium

Joseph Lee

War Poet and Artist

'Of the verse that has come straight from the trenches, the BALLADS OF BATTLE are among the very best. The horror, the exultation, the weariness, and the humour of trench warfare are here.'

The Spectator

RANKED ALONGSIDE Owen, Brooke and Sassoon, Joseph Lee was once regarded as one of Scotland's finest First World War poets. During the conflict his works were well known in Britain and America and were read as far afield as New Zealand. Although his reputation has since been sadly eclipsed, his poetry and war memoirs remain powerfully evocative and are undeniably authentic. What makes Lee more remarkable is that he was also a highly skilled artist who illustrated his own books and, after the war, moved to London to study at the Slade alongside the likes of Stanley Spencer.

Lee was born in Dundee in 1876. The son of a draper's assistant and one of nine siblings, Lee and his family lived in a cramped tenement. The town at this time was an expanding industrial centre with a rapidly growing population, from under 64,000 in 1841 to over 153,000 by 1891. Its economy was principally driven by the jute and flax industry and massive textile mills with large chimneys dominated the landscape. Also crucial to the town was the busy port where ships from across the British Empire and the wider world came to trade, and which, along with the growing railway network, served as Dundee's main connection with the outside world. Within a few years of Lee's birth Dundee underwent significant changes. Industry had brought new wealth to Dundee, but it had also left many of its citizens living in appalling housing conditions. The years around the late nineteenth century saw attempts to 'improve' the city, the fabric of which had suffered greatly from the population expansions of the previous decade. However the programme of rebuilding had mixed results at best as many areas of bad housing were untouched while some notable buildings were sacrificed in the name of modernity. The conditions in which some of his fellow Dundonians lived and worked seem to have affected the young Lee deeply, as his later writings show.

Joseph Lee was an intelligent child but, as with most children from an underprivileged background, staying in education was not an option when he could be earning a wage for his family. Thus he left school at 14 to work for a firm of local solicitors. Finding this career uninspiring he began attending art classes at the local YMCA and he spent some time travelling through Europe and the Black Sea, working and sketching and even, in 1901 or 1902, spending the summer as a cowboy on cattle ranch in Canada. By 1904 Lee was working as a cartoonist in London and undertaking further study at Heatherley's School of Fine Art. Drawing and sketching was becoming his passion; he later wrote that he always saw himself as an artist masquerading as a poet and journalist but he gradually realised that the pen was mightier than the pencil.

In 1906 Lee returned to Dundee where he worked on a number of publications including the *People's Journal* and the *Dundee Advertiser*. He also wrote, edited and illustrated the magazines *The City Echo* and *The Piper o' Dundee*. The city had a reputation for journalism and publishing with the firms of John Leng and D.C. Thomson being significant figures in the newspaper and periodical world. Although by 1906 the Leng business had been acquired by Thomson, both firms, along with several smaller concerns, continued to produce a diverse range of publications some of which competed with each other.

Thus Dundee was fertile ground for a would-be journalist and artist. *The City Echo* and *The Piper o' Dundee* were wide-ranging in their coverage and as well as providing local news they addressed a variety of social and political themes. Politics in Dundee, as across the UK, was volatile at this time and Lee drew many cartoons tackling such issues as female suffrage and Irish Home Rule. Among those featured (and indeed targeted) were Winston Churchill, Liberal MP for the city from 1908, and the Prohibitionist Councillor Edwin 'Neddy' Scrymgeour, who would later go on to defeat Churchill. Lee's love of the arts also shone through in both titles, not least through their coverage of local entertainment.

One of Lee's most interesting periodicals was the 1909 monthly *The Tocsin*. This promoted the work of the Labour Party and its affiliates and received praise from a number of senior figures in the labour movement, including Keir Hardie who lauded its 'high class journalism'. Although Dundee had traditionally

'A woman, with wildly-staring but unseeing eyes, with dark coils of Medusa hair, and with a face that might well Gorgonise one into stone, staggers across the street.' — *In Darkest Dundee, sketch by Lee from The City Echo*

been a stronghold of liberalism, the Labour Party was on the rise in the city and in 1906 Alexander Wilkie captured one of the two Dundee parliamentary seats to become Scotland's first Labour MP. As well as offering an insight into the Labour Party's activities *The Tocsin* contained many articles on political and social themes as well as literary essays. The paper ceased publication after less than a year, possibly in part due to libellous remarks it printed about a parish councillor. Nevertheless Lee and *The Tocsin* played an important part in building up the party's support in Dundee.

Lee's literary and artistic talent was given wider recognition with the publication of his first book of poetry, *Tales o' our Town*, in 1910, enhanced by his own illustrations. Lee further demonstrated his literary versatility by writing and acting in a one-act play, *The Song: An Episode from Bohemia*, which was performed at Her Majesty's Theatre in 1913. He followed this up with a longer play entitled *Fra Lippo Lippi* dramatising the life of the Florentine painter and friar made famous by Robert Browning. It was staged in 1914 by staff and students at Dundee School of Art, the predecessor of today's Duncan of Jordanstone College of Art and Design.

Just a few months later war was declared and Lee enlisted in the 4th Battalion of the Black Watch, known as 'Dundee's Ain'. Lee's actions were to some extent surprising. Many of his former associates in the labour movement were opposed to the war and, in his late 30s and asthmatic, Lee was far from being in peak fighting condition. Possibly he was partly inspired by his grandfather, Sergeant David Lee, who had fought at Waterloo and who was later the subject of Lee's poem '1815-1915, One Hundred Years Ago Today'. Equally he may have got swept up in the wave of patriotism and enthusiasm for the cause that enveloped much of Dundee. Whatever the case, he probably did not realise that the pivotal moment in his literary career had come.

Lee, like many thousands of Scots, soon experienced at

first hand the horrors of warfare in France and Belgium. With other members of the 4th Black Watch he left Dundee for France in February 1915 and saw service in many major battles including Neuve Chapelle, Loos and the Somme. He proved to be a good and reliable soldier and companion and was promoted to sergeant before being commissioned as an officer in 1917. In a series of articles in the *Evening Telegraph* in 1930 one of his fellow soldiers referred to Lee as 'One of the best loved men in the company. There was nothing Joe would not do for a comrade if it was in his power. Above all in France he kept us cheerful in our platoon, because when he was with us no matter how filthy was the trench scene and how nauseous the smell of the dead and its butcher duties he never let us forget the background of civilised life; he was our link with great minds and great art and the pure pleasures of the mind.'

Lee found expression for his experiences in his sketches and poetry, which were sent home and exhibited in the Albert Institute (now The McManus: Dundee's Art Gallery & Museum) and published in the *Dundee Advertiser*. His first book of war poetry, *Ballads of Battle*, was published in April 1916 while he was still at the front, and received favourable reviews both in Britain and in the United States. *The Times* stated that there was 'real fibre and lifeblood' in the poems, adding that 'they never fail to hold the attention.' *The Guardian* considered *Ballads* to be 'one of the most striking publications of the war'. The New York publication *Every-week* asked in its review 'Who is this new poet?' before going on to praise his work as 'true poetry; genuine in feeling, perfectly unconventional, intensely personal. Here is one of the best'. In December that year *The Scotsman* named Lee, Rupert Brooke and A.P. Herbert as the most popular poets of the war. The success of the poems was such that a selection were set to music by J.F. Heyde and printed as a song book. Lee's next volume, *Work-A-Day Warriors*, published in 1917, was equally well received with *The Scotsman* praising his verse for the impression it conveyed of a soldier's life at the front and noting that his illustrations added 'not a

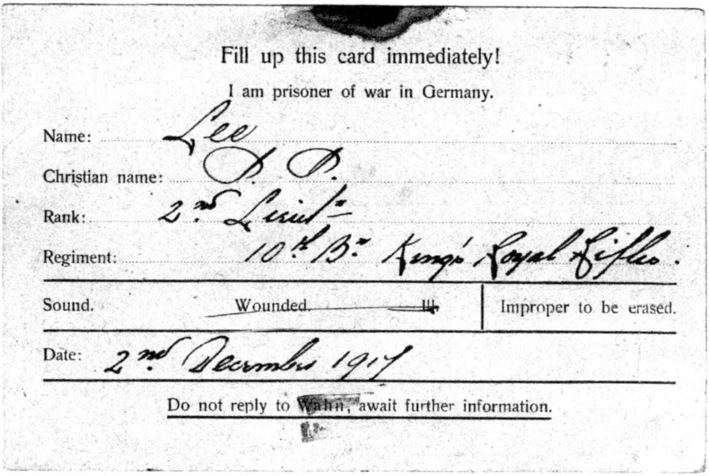

Fill up this card immediately!

I am prisoner of war in Germany.

Name: Lee

Christian name: D. P.

Rank: 2nd Lieut.

Regiment: 10th Bn. Kings Royal Rifles.

Sound. ~~Wounded.~~ | Improper to be erased.

Date: 2nd December 1917

Do not reply to [redacted], await further information.

little' to the strength of the text. The book was significant enough to be reviewed by *The New York Times* which, while critical of Lee's choice of title, praised his writing.

Having been present at bloody fighting on the battlefields of Loos and Ypres, Lee's luck appeared to run out at the end of November 1917 when he was reported as missing in action at the Battle of Cambrai. However, a short time later his family were informed that he had been taken prisoner. Lee was first taken by his captors to Caudry, then Le Cateau, before being moved to Karlsruhe camp in Germany where he joined officers from seventeen different nations. Despite numerous attempts, no one ever managed to escape from Karlsruhe. En route, Lee had persuaded one of his captors to buy him a sketchbook and pencil and after careful scrutiny he was allowed to retain his drawings and sketch freely within the camp. To keep themselves entertained the prisoners created their own theatre where they performed plays and staged musical concerts. The multi-talented Lee soon found himself pressed into service as 'scene-painter, scene-shifter, poster-artist, actor, prompter, "noises-off," and playwright.' One of Lee's fellow prisoners, who was repatriated on medical grounds during the war, described him as 'the one redeeming feature of the place'. Lee also recorded his experience of camp life in diaries illustrated with photographs and sketches of prisoners, guards and his surroundings. These were published in October 1920 as the book *A Captive in Carlsruhe.*

In July 1918 Lee was moved to another camp at Beeskow. Here security was much more lax, a parole system allowing Lee to wander unaccompanied into town and sketch his surroundings. It was clear the war was nearly over. When the Armistice was declared Lee was not immediately released but the prisoners were allowed further liberties. In early December 1918, Lee and a fellow prisoner visited Berlin where, amongst excursions to cafes and sightseeing trips, he watched a Spartacist procession headed by Rosa Luxemburg and Karl Liebknecht.

On his return to Beeskow Lee was formally released and after briefly returning to Dundee he moved to London, where he renewed his acquaintance with the young viola player Dorothy Barrie. The couple were married in Dundee in 1924 and then settled in Epsom. Lee kept writing into the 1920s, but

his last major poem was 'A Northern Town', published in the University College, Dundee students' anthology *The New Meal Poke* in 1922. Subsequently he concentrated on journalism, becoming sub-editor for the *News Chronicle*, a major national newspaper. He also returned to art, attending classes at the Slade School of Fine Art. During this period he encountered and sketched many famous figures including Edward Elgar, John Barbirolli, Edith Sitwell, Stanley Spencer and Max Beerbohm. Lee again served his country in the Second World War, this time as a member of the Home Guard from 1940 to 1944. He returned to Dundee shortly before his death in 1949.

Many of Lee's drawings, publications, papers and photographs are held in the University of Dundee's archive and museum collections. They provide a fascinating glimpse of his experiences and of life in the early part of the twentieth century. Of particular value are the diaries Lee kept while a prisoner of war containing a wealth of detail about life in the camps, complete with photographs, drawings and ephemera. The collection also includes correspondence about Lee's poetry (including his literary argument with the Poet Laureate Robert Bridges over the merits of Robert Burns), journals covering the Second World War and his life in London during the Blitz, life drawings done as a student at the Slade, and many of the original illustrations for his books.

Caroline Brown
Matthew Jarron
Kenneth Baxter
University of Dundee Archive and Museum Services

Lee's Poetry

WAR POET AND ARTIST, Joseph Lee, widely known at the time as 'Dundee's Battle Bard', unaccountably disappeared from the post-Great War canon. Perhaps the key reason is because Lee's work is so hard to categorise, both aesthetically and politically. He neither settled into becoming a poet of outright protest, undergoing a process of bitter disillusionment with the conduct of the war and the purity of British motives like Sassoon or Owen; nor was Lee a naïve patriot or mere propagandist - his work displayed a sense of the accumulating ironies of personal and national loss and, therefore, an ever-more poignant awareness that the common soldier's sacrifice was redeemable only if it had truly been necessary and unavoidable.

Lee was a keen observer of daily life in the trenches and the almost surreal domesticity prevailing between bouts of action; his poetry focuses as much on the camaraderie and humour as the mayhem and horror. Lee was most at home in the 'dramatic monologue' or soliloquy form, which Tennyson and Browning perfected for drawing readers into imagining situations they had not experienced directly themselves. He was also a vocal chameleon, gliding skilfully between personae and registers: from Standard English and Burnsian Scots ('The Haggis', 'I Canna See the Sergeant'), to Kiplingesque 'mockney' reminiscent of Barrack Room Ballads ('Glad that I Killed Yer', 'The Things I've Seen').

No doubt Lee's own youthful exploits on the North American plains tuned his ear to the Alberta vernacular he also renders so vividly in 'War: Some Reflections by Corporal Richard Crew of the Canadians'. Crew had no time for the 'poet-soldiers' like

Rupert Brooke who romanticised the allied cause before seeing action, whatever he might have come to think of experienced 'soldier-poets' like Lee: 'No, War ain't what them long-haired coves/Have cracked it up to be!' Although Lee puts the following words in Crew's mouth, the reader can't help wondering whether it is Lee himself, artist's eye rendering the full palette of war experience in all its darkness and occasional light, who is really characterised by them: 'I guess there are/Redeeming tints to war'.

Lee's testimonial 'The Things I've Seen' is a spectrum of the absurdities and randomness that could throw trench life into both tragic and humanising relief almost simultaneously: sharing a friendly cigarette with a prisoner you were trying to bayonet moments before; watching doomed air-crew struggling not to crash in slow-motion; hearing larksong in brief interludes of quiet during a deafening barrage ('An earthquake held in leash'); seeing the cosmic indifference of seasonal processes and weather to the dividing lines between belligerents. In 'The Penitent', Lee pokes witty, but warmly empathic fun at frontline conversations based on bargaining with the Almighty going over the top. Having apparently survived 'Noove Chapelle' through promising to renounce alcohol and other pleasures of the flesh which make the Tommy's routine more endurable, Lee's speaker admits relapse is inevitable once the pressure's off. 'The Haggis', a comic poem about ritual consumption of Scotland's national dish at the Front, requires careful contextualisation in the mindset of the time; otherwise its cheery metaphors of disembowelment may make us wince too much:

"A British bayonet's jag is
The Best for Hun or Haggis!"
Wi' that he straightway falls on it
And gie'es the Haggis sic a slit;
The whereupon, entrancing sight,
The hidden glories come to light....

'Glad that I Killed Yer: A Modern Song of Lamech', as its title suggests, expresses Lee's sense of the war as a regrettable struggle to the death between common soldiers who mutually respect each other on both sides. Lee in no way glorifies hand-to-hand experience of what W.H. Auden would later call (from a purely theoretical distance) 'necessary murder'. On the other hand, 'The Bullet', perhaps Lee's best known short verse, reflects a different perspective on the ethics of killing even when the patriotic duty seems clear. The poem displays Lee's technical craft at its most deceptively simple, with brilliant assonance between 'bullet' and 'billet'. Lee turns the familiar name for a Tommy's cosy, improvised lodging into the body his fatal shot lodges in. The idea that a single cartridge impacts several

times over, through the trauma inflicted on the enemy's family behind the lines, also unleashes an emotional 'ricochet' for the speaker – an incurable wound in the memory of his killer.

In 'Our British Dead', Lee vocalises the fallen into apparently unanimous endorsement of the national cause for which they perished en masse: 'Here do we lie, dead but not discontent,/That which we found to do has had accomplishment.' But other poems revisit the theme from more troubled perspectives. 'The Green Grass' was Lee's own deeply moving version of the ironic pastoral that became common, as poets tried to reconcile the sodden, body-strewn fields of the Western Front with memories of tranquil rural landscapes at home. In effect, 'The Green Grass' is a kind of 'dialogue of the dead' in which those lying, buried underground lament aspects of everyday, civilian life which continues above without them. Perhaps not as directly as Owen or Sassoon, but no less poignantly, the poem calls the living to account, implicitly asking whether the heroic sacrifice of so many was indeed necessary or justifiable. Lee's is a more subtle, but no less haunting version of the question posed by Abel Gance's zombie army that rises from mass graves at the end of his film, *J'Accuse* (1919). Such uncanny visions remained common in the War's aftermath, as in Irwin Shaw's 1936 play *Bury the Dead*, in which its casualties similarly refuse to obey the order to lie down and be quiet.

The 'Half-Hour's Furlough' shows Lee capable of the most haunting lyricism. The speaker's yearning consciousness leaves the night-time trenches to wander familiar streets of home, finding temporary solace in a vision of maternal blessing before being rudely shocked back to the here and now by the 'stand to arms'. Similarly, for sheer eeriness 'The Listening Post' is unmatchable. A soldier at a forward position in no-man's land struggles not to believe that the surrounding dead are also spying on him in return. 'Ancestry' is another kind of vision (illustrated by Lee's sketch "Tank" in Action), superimposing this most modern of wars onto scenarios of conflict stretching back to the Stone Age. The speaker feels united with the anonymous common warriors of the past and the future in both their prowess and their human vulnerability.

For this and many more merits too numerous for a brief introduction, we believe readers of this anthology will find the work of Joseph Lee deserves to be re-discovered and to be returned to its rightful place in the canon of Great War poetry.

Keith Williams
University of Dundee School of Humanities

YPRES–CHRISTMAS EVE

"Glad That I Killed Yer"

A Modern Song of Lamech

Hear my voice; hearken unto my speech: for I
Have slain a man. – Genesis iv. 23.

Glad that I killed yer—
It was you or me:
Our bayonets locked,
And then I pulled mine free;
My heart beat like to burst;
But Gawd, I got in first—
Glad that I killed yer!

Glad that I killed yer,
Though you are so young:
How still you lie
With both your arms outflung:
There's red blood on your hair—
Well, what the Hell I care?
Glad that I killed yer!

Glad that I killed yer—
You're my enemy;
I had to hate—
And you—you hated me;
You mightn't be to blame—
I killed yer just the same—
Glad that I killed yer!

Glad that I killed yer—
That's the game o' war;
But for my luck

I'd lie just like you are;
Your blood is on my hand—
Surely you understand
I *had* to kill yer?

Glad that I killed yer—
Yet I can't forget
The look you gave me
When we turned—and met—
Why do you follow me with staring
eye?
Was it so difficult a thing to die—
Gawd! when *I* killed yer?

Glad that I killed yer—
Yet I'm sorry, too,
For those will wait
So long at home for you:
I have a mother living down at
Bow—
Thank Gawd for this that yours
will never know
'Twas I that killed yer!

Glad that I killed yer—
It was you or me:
It does seem strange,
But it had got to be.
My heart beat like to burst,
But Gawd, I got in first—
Glad that I killed yer!

The Green Grass

The dead spake together last night,
And one to the other said:
"Why are we dead?"

They turned them face to face about
In the place where they were laid:
"Why are we dead?"

"This is the sweet, sweet month o' May,
And the grass is green o'erhead—
Why are we dead?

"The grass grows green on the long, long tracks
That I shall never tread—
Why are we dead?"

"The lamp shines like the glow-worm spark,
From the bield where I was bred—
Why am I dead?"

The other spake: "I've wife and weans,
Yet I lie in this waesome bed—
Why am I dead?

"O, I hae wife and weans at hame,
And they clamour loud for bread—
Why am I dead?"

Quoth the first: "I have a sweet, sweet heart,
And this night we should hae wed—
Why am I dead?

"And I can see another man
Will mate her in my stead,
Now I am dead."

They turned them back to back about
In the grave where they were laid:—
"Why are we dead?"

"I mind o' a field, a foughten field,
Where the bluid ran routh and red—
Now I am dead."

"I mind o' a field, a stricken field,
And a waeful wound that bled—
Now I am dead."

They turned them on their backs again,
As when their souls had sped,
And nothing further said.

* * * *

The dead spake together last night,
And each to the other said,
"Why are we dead?"

Our British Dead

O stranger, bring the Spartans word, that here,
Obedient thus to their command, we lie.
Simonides

Here do we lie, dead but not discontent,
That which we found to do has had
accomplishment.

No more for us uprise or set of sun;
The vigilant night, the desperate day is
done.

To other hands we leave the avenging
sword,
To other tongues to speak the arousing
word.

Here do we lie, dead but not discontent,
That which was ours to do has had
accomplishment.

Forget us not, O Land for which we fell—
May it go well with England, still go well.

Keep her bright banners without blot or
stain,
Lest we should dream that we have died
in vain.

Brave be the days to come, when we
Are but a wistful memory….

Here do we lie, dead but not discontent,
That which we found to do has had
    accomplishment.

'SOMEWHERE IN FRANCE'

"I Canna See The Sergeant"

Those readers who have recollection of the drilling days of the 4th Battalion Black Watch may remember to have heard some words—often, fortunately, not entirely intelligible—which we rendered lustily as a marching song, to the Gaelic melody, "Horo My Nut-Brown Maiden." In these strenuous and sad times the phrase, "I Canna See the Sergeant," which formed the owre-turn o' the sang, has often assumed a new and deeper significance.

I canna see the sergeant,
I canna see the sergeant,
I canna—see the—sergeant,*
He's owre far awa'.
Bring the wee chap nearer,
Bring the wee chap nearer,
O bring the—wee chap—nearer—
He's owre bloomin' sma'.

We canna see the sergeant,
The five foot five inch sergeant,
We canna—see the—sergeant
For smoke, and shell, and a'—
Now we can see him clearer,
Now we can see him nearer—
Upon the topmost parapet
He's foremost o' us a'!

We canna see the sergeant,
The sma', stout-hearted sergeant,
We canna—see the—sergeant,

***To be sung in staccato fashion.**

He's dead and gone awa'.
Bring the wee chap nearer,
Bring the wee chap nearer,
O, he has grown the dearer
Now that he's far awa'!

'EACH FLAG SHOWED THE PALE FACE OF DEFEAT'

Leave

He was going home to-morrow, his heart
was light and gay;
He was going home to-morrow—but he
went Home to-day!

SOLDIERS SHELTERING IN A CELLAR DURING A HEAVY BOMBARDMENT

The Drum

'Come to me and I will give you flesh.'
Old Pibrochadh

Come!
Says the drum;
        Though graves be hollow,
        Yet follow, follow:
Come!
Says the drum.

Life!
Shrills the fife,
Is in strife—
Leave love and wife:
Come!
Says the drum.

Ripe!
Screams the pipe,
        Is the field—
        Swords and not sickles wield:
Come!
Says the drum.

The drum
Says, Come!
        Though graves be hollow,
        Yet follow, follow:
Come!
Says the drum.

TYPICAL BARN BILLET

War

Some Reflections by
Corporal Richard Crew of the Canadians

From whence come wars and fightings? - James iv. I.

SURE, I dunno;
There's some men call War "murder,"
Some say it's elevatin';
I've 'eard both sides
Their cases statin'
An hour or so—
But I dunno.

There was Jim,
Got blown up in a mine:
He was elevated right enough—
But yet I felt it tough,
For I was fond o' him.
And then, pore Jake,
Struck in 's stummach,
Went swearin' straight to hell—
If hell ain't all a fake—
No, siree, War
Ain't pretty like a Calendar!

One thing—the dead
Ain't beautifully spread,
Each with an artistic scar
'Cross his fore'ead;
No, that ain't War
Whatever poets say—

Shrapnel and high explosive
Do not work that way.

Ye mind o' Ned?—
Him what went West
At St. Eloi?—
A rare good boy,
One o' the very best;
Well, *his* pore 'ead
Was blown clean off,
And biffed me in the chest!—
It seems to me
There's something in the murder theory.

I've been out 'ere
Just on two year,
And seen it all
From Wipers to the Somme;
And not much bugle blowing,
Nor banner flowing,
And all that truck;
Just mostly muck and mud,
And mud and muck,
And what the Frenchies call, I think,
ang-wee;
No, War ain't what them long-haired
coves
Have cracked it up to be!

And yet,
You bet,
There's something in it, too—
Not gauged by me and you;
My Gawd, I've stood
After a heavy biff,
Pondering a bit on death—

And getting back my breath—
Thinking how boys have died,
Until, by Christ, I've cried—
Yet, somehow it seemed GOOD!

I mind me how
Just night the Hat[1]—
(Wish was there now!)
We rounded up a snake—
Some rattler at that!
And Lariat Jack
Bent o'er his saddle bow
And gripped the rattler so,
And broke its bloomin' back,
And I said "Shake,"
And yet felt sorry, too,
For that there worm
Was wondrous beautiful of hue!

I guess there are
Redeeming tints to War.
Mayhap the Lord—
Who makes the silly snakes,
And breathes in storm, and shakes
The everlastin' hills wi' His earth-
quakes;
Who sets a little lamb
Upon an English mead,
Yet lets the tiger breed
And the wolf dam
Down in the jungle—

[1] *Medicine Hat, a town in Alberta, which derives its name—for the retention of which Rudyard Kipling made an eloquent and successful plea with his pen—from the fact that, seven Indians having been drowned higher up the creek, the hat of the Medicine Man here floated up. By the Cow-puncher it is designated colloquially and affectionately "The Hat". Wish I had my head in it now!*

Mayhap the Lord
        Ain't made no bloomin' bungle,
But even in bloody war—
Such as this are—
    Fulfils His wondrous Word!

Christ! I am cold, wish Sergeant Wood
    would come,
And dish me out my morning tot o' rum!

MACFARLANE IN HIS DUG-OUT
A Portrait Sketch

The Haggis

To Mrs M—, to whom we were indebted for a haggis,
whose amplitude was in somewise commensurate
with the largeness of her heart.

Fair fa' your honest, sonsie face,
Great chieftain o' the pudding race!

A Haggis; a Haggis,
An honest Scottish Haggis!
Let Frenchmen make a loud to-do
About the length o' their menu—
New-fangled fricassee, ragout,
And sic like dishes—
Auld Scotia's simple brag is
Her ancient Haggis!

To me arrives a Haggis;
A Haggis?—A HAGGIS!
A healthy, wholesome Haggis
As ever ye did see,
And writ upon the tag is:
"To Sergeant Joseph Lee—
Just boil it for a wee!"

Ah! well kenn'd I wha made it—
Frae the foundation laid it—
Wha packed it up, and prayed it
Wad in condition be—
As tho' hersel' had said it—
It brought me memorie
O' the land sae dear to me—

Land where the rock and crag is,
Land where the rill and quag is,
Land where the leaping stag is—
Did this Scotch Haggis.

"Go out into the highways,
Go out into the byways,"
    Quo' I in muckle glee,
"Go into ilka billet—
The fatted calf is kille't—
And say that so we will it—
    Compel them come and pree
The big and buirdly Haggis
    That's been sent out to me!"
"Losh, but I'll sound the slogan!"
Cried souple Stievie Logan,
    And aff at aince set he.

The Haggis; THE Haggis,
Yes, let us to the Haggis—
Pegasus, my nag is
    Inclined to need the spur—
We passed it for inspection,
    Then in the pot
Till it was hot—
O, glorious resurrection!

The Haggis, the Haggis;
Wull Wright an unco' wag is,
    And he cried out wi' passion,
      "The smell itsel'
      Might very well
Serve for a sodger's ration!"
Now quick the Cook arrays it,
And in the Piper plays it;
    Ye never heard siccan a din,

The billet roof came tumblin' in.
(I dinna ken wha pays it—
That's quite anither story.)
Dan gi'es us "Scotland's Glory";
His ruddy cheeks are outward blawn,
His neb is cocked, his neck is
thrawn,
He blaws until his bag is
As big's our muckle Haggis!

Behind him, Billy Milne, elate,
Bears the great chieftain on a plate,
Advancing and retiring—
Like the Haggis' sel' perspiring—
Wi' many a step frae many a dance
Unknown in the salons o' France.
Now, round and round the room they go
For it is seemly even so;
At last amidst the babel
The Haggis takes the table!
The guests await, the Grace is said,
Then the proud host outdraws his blade:
"A British bayonet's jag is
The best for Hun or Haggis!"
Wi' that he straightaway falls on it
And gi'es the Haggis sic a slit;
The whereupon, entrancing sight,
The hidden glories come to light—
"Advance, attack, each valiant wight,
And make good play wi' fork and spoon,
The Devil take the hindmost done—
The first to fail or flag is
No' worthy o' a Haggis!"

No need to force a Scotsman go
To find a friend or fight a foe,

And swiftly at that given word
They fall on it wi' one accord,
Wi' spoon and gully-knife and fork
They make the shortest o' short work–
There's ne'er been sic a stabbin'
Since our boys took the Schwaben!
They hack and hew that Haggis
Till a' that's left a rag is!
And when they've worked their will o't,
And when they've ate their fill o't,
Mair nor ae chield can scarcely drag his
Sel' frae that feast o' Haggis!

A Haggis, a Haggis,
An honest, homely Haggis!–
Land where the riven crag is,
Land where the leaping stag is,
Thy proudest boast and brag is
Thy ancient Haggis!

The Bullet

Every bullet has its billet;
    Many bullets more than one:
God! Perhaps I killed a mother
    When I killed a mother's son.

SUBIDAR MAJOR JOCUNDAR SINGH
69th PUNJABIS

The Things I've Seen

Perhaps a hundred years from now,
When I below the sod am jammed,
Some bloke may pick up this 'ere pome,
And read, and say, "Well, I'll be
damned!"

"There's nothing new," the Preacher says,
"That happens underneath the sun"—
And yet the curious things I've seen;
The bloomin' curious things I've done.

I've seen young blokes what has been bred
To sell duds in a draperie,
Stand under fire and keep their head
Wi' seasoned sodjers same as me!

I've 'ad them on a bombing raid,
Wi' faces and wi' bay'nets black,
And not a single one afraid
And not a single man hang back!

They've lain and waited till the wire
Was cut and scattered by our shells,
Then waltzed into the German trench
As gay as Negro minster-els!

I've seen our Batt. go singing in
To what was well-nigh certain death;
I've seen 'em die, and heard 'em cheer
For Britain wi' their dying breath!

I've seen my matey standing by,
    And asked him if a fag he'd got;
He hadn't even time to cry
    When something took him—*he was not!*

I've seen a bloke shot thro' the head—
    A bloke I ne'er heard swear afore—
He spun right round, and dropped down
    dead,
And wot he said was, "O you whore!"

I've seen me chargin' on the foe,
    To prod him wi' my bayonet;
Then "Kamerad!" – and next I know
    I'm handing him a cigarette!

I've seen our sappers spring a mine,
    That darkened all the sky at noon,
And left a hole within their line
    Like some lorn crater of the moon!

I've seen the Germans shell a town,
    In this ungracious year o' grace;
A market town, on market day –
    And first shell in the market-place!

I've seen an aeroplane brought down,
    Just like a bird wi' broken wing,
And watched, for what seemed like a week,
    Them doomed men try to right the
        thing!

I've heard the guns at Neuve Chapelle –
    An earthquake held in leash, say I,
Yet o'er the hubbub of that hell,
    I've heard a lark sing in the sky!

I've seen, amidst this waste o' war,
    God's goodly seasons come and go;
And flowers bloom in the wilderness,
    And rain fall both on friend and foe.

I've seen—I've seen a heap o' things,
    That I ain't got no time to tell,
But every word is Gospel true—
    I've done most o' the things mysel',

"All vanity," the Preacher says,
    "There's nothing new beneath the
    sun"—
And still the curious things I've seen,
    The amazing curious things I've done!

Perchance a hundred years from now,
    When I below the sod am jammed,
Some bloke will pick up this 'ere pome,
    And read, and say, "Well, I'll be
        damned!"

And say!—If for the hist'ry books,
    Some o' my words seem rather warm,
Perhaps some bloke might sort 'em out—
    I wouldn't do the kids no harm!

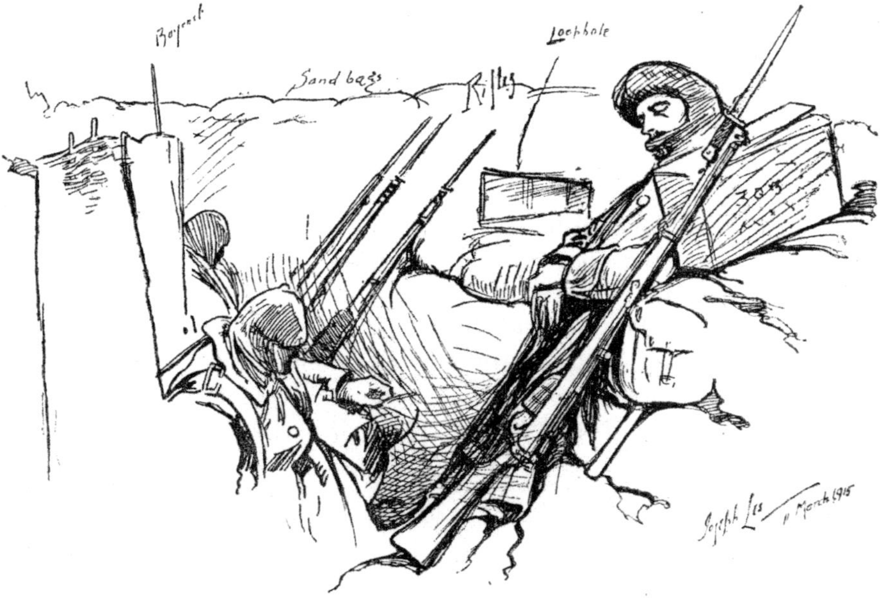

DAWN IN THE TRENCHES

An unfinished drawing made on the morning after Neuve Chapelle

As Lazarus risen from the dead. – "At the Dawn"

The Penitent

As I lay in the trenches at Noove Chapelle,
Where the big guns barked like the
  Hounds o' Hell,
Sez I to mysel', sez I to mysel': --

Billy, me boy, here's the end o' you—
But if, by good luck, ye should chance to
  slip thro',
Ye'll bid all ye'r evil companions adieu;
Keep the Lord's ten Commandments—and
  Lord Kitchener's two—
      Sez I to mysel'—at Noove Chapelle.

No more women, and no more wine,
No more hedgin' to get down the line,
No more hoggin' around like a swine,
      After Noove Chapelle—sez I to mysel',
But only the good God in Heaven knows
The wayward way that a soldier goes,
And He must ha' left me to walk by my-
  sel'—
      For three times I've fell, since Noove
        Chapelle.

Once at Bethune and twice at Estaires,
The divil gripped hould o' me unawares—
Yet often and often I've prayed me prayers,
      Since I prayed by mysel', at Noove
        Chapelle.

Well, the Lord above, who fashioned the
French,
May bethink how bewitchin' is wine and a
wench
To a chap that's been tied for three weeks
to a trench,
Around Noove Chapelle—that black
border o' Hell.

And me throat was dry and the night was
damp,
And the rum was raw—and red was the
lamp!—
And—Billy, me boy, ye'r a bit o' a scamp,
That's the truth to tell—tho' I sez it mysel'.

What's worritin' me isn't fear that they'll
miss
Me out o' the ranks in the realms o' bliss;
It ain't hope o' Heaven, nor horror o' Hell,
But just breakin' the promise, 'twixt God
and mysel',
Made at Noove Chapelle.

Well, there's always a way that is open to
men
When they gets the knock-out—that's get
up again;
And, sure now, ould Satan ain't yet
counted ten!
I'm game for another good bout wi' my-
sel'—
As at Noove Chapelle.

Trench Thoughts

Christmas 1916

Not of the Christ who came
Two thousand years ago;
Only the firelight glow
In one loved cot I know.

Not of those shepherds old,
Watching their flocks by night!
But Father, and Kate with a light,
Seeing that cows is right.

Not of the Angel song;
Peace unto men of Goodwill;
Only my brother Bill
Dead, and he done no ill!

Not of the Heavenly Host,
Bringing tidings of great joy;
But my Mother's homely employ,
And her prayer, "My boy, my boy!"

A GHOST STORY AT THE FRONT

A tale, let's say, both weird and fierce
By Allan Poe or Ambrose Bierce

– "The Billet"

The Half-Hour's Furlough

I thought that a man went home last
night
From the trench where the tired men
lie,
And walked through the streets of his own
old town—
And I thought that the man was I.

And I walked through the gates of that
good old town
Which circles below the hill,
And laves its feet in the river fair
That floweth so full and still.

Gladly and gladly into my heart
Came the old street sounds and sights,
And pleasanter far than the Pleiades
Was the gleam of the old street lights.

And as I came by St. Mary's Tower,
The old, solemn bell struck ten,
And back to me echoed the memory
Of my boyhood days again:
Musing I turned me East about
To the haunt of my fellow-men.

There were some that walked, and some
that talked,
Beneath the old Arcade,
And for comfort I elbowed among the
throng
And hearkened to what they said.

Some were that talked, and some that
walked
By one, by two, by three;
And some there were who spake my name
As though they loved me.

And some who said, "Might he but return
When this weary war is spent!"
And it moved me much that their thought
was such,
And I turned me well content.

I passed me along each familiar way,
And paused at each friendly door,
And thought of the things that had
chanced within
In the kindly days of yore.

Till I came to the place of my long, long
love,
Where she lay with her head on her arm;
And she sighed a prayer that the dear
Lord should
Shield my body from all harm.

Ae kiss I left on her snow-white brow,
And ane on her raven hair,
And ane, the last, on her ruby lips,
Syne forth again I fare.

And I came to the home that will aye be
home,
And brightly the fires did burn,
And at hearth, and in hearts, was a place
for me
'Gainst the day that I should return.

Then I came to the glade where my mother
 was laid,
 'Neath the cypress and the yew:
And she stood abune, and she said, "My
 son,
I am glad that your heart was true."

And I passed me over both hill and down,
 By each well-remembered path,
While the blessed dawn, like the love o'
 God,
 Stole over the sleeping Strath.

And from a thorn came the pipe of a
 thrush,
 Like the first faint pipes of Peace:
It slid with healing into my heart,
 And my sorrowing found surcease.

* * *

Then I awoke to the sound of guns,
 And in my ears was the cry:
"The Second Relief will stand to arms!"
 And I rose—for that man was I.

VIA DOLOROSA

Bringing in the wounded after 9th May

Carrying-Party

Time 10.30pm. Place, Communication Trenches.

WIRE over'ead!
Mud underfoot:
Gawd, I'm into a hole,
Pullin' the sole
Right off'en me boot—
I wish I was dead!

Wire over'ead—
(My load weighs like lead)
The night's black as 'ell;
I'm into a ditch—
Ye son of a bitch!
'Twas here Nelson fell—
Bang! There goes a shell—
I wish I was dead!

Wire over'ead!—
Look out for the bridge!
Hear ole Sergeant grunt,
"Halt! you there in the front!
They've lost touch at the ridge"—
I wish *I* was dead!

Wire over'ead!
Wire underfoot!—
There's Tim come to grief—
Christ!—he's dumping the beef.
Pull 'im out by the root:
I wish I was dead—
(To home blokes are in bed)—
Wish Gawd I was dead!
(Stumbles and grumbles on.)

INTERIOR OF THE BARN

– "The Billet."

The Listening Post

Four live men lie in the grass,
Listening what may come to pass;
Open eye, attentive ear –
Four dead men are lying near.

We four lying in the rain,
Hearkening if perchance we gain
Inkling of our enemy –
That dead hand seemed to beckon me!

We four 'neath the lowering sky;
Straining ear, and open eye;
A star-shell lights a ghostly cheek –
Hark! did I hear that dead man speak?

Out beneath the blackened sky
We four listening live men lie;
Deep into the dark we peer –
And four dead men seem watching near!

Unto the earth my ear I keep;
I hear her breathing, long and deep;
The speeding shadows come and go –
Is that patrol friend or foe?

Beneath the blackened heavens we lie,
Three brave lads — *the dead* — and I;
Open eye—attentive ear—
They do not hear the sounds I hear,
Nor see four dead men watching near!

"TANK" IN ACTION

Ancestry

I AM one with my fleet-foot forebear,
skin-clad, with his flint-head spear;
I am one with the savage tribesman,
with his bow-string taut to his ear;
I am one with them in their courage;
one with them in their fear:
As I lie out here, with dead men near
In this Listening-Post with my gun
They and I are One!

I am one with the ancient Roman,
pressing on in his grim phalanx;
I am one with the Spartan, the Trojan,
and the Grecian's steel-clad ranks;
They with their Horse, Heaven-sent,
and I with my earth-born "tanks";
As I move to attack, with my kit on my
back,
And my bombs and my steel-tipped
gun,
They and I are One!

I am one with the cohorts of Caesar;
with the hosts of Hannibal;
With the legions of all the leaders
to the last "Petit Caporal";
One with the millions of nameless dead,
who have fallen as soldiers fall:
As I crawl through the breach in the
battered wall,
Or charge at the run with my gun,
They and I are One!

By black hearths in the broken farm.
– "When We Remembered —"

"When We Remembered—"

Think not, far friends, that we forget,
In these red realms of wrack and rue,
The white cliffs round our England set,
The Channel waters white and blue.

Think not, that on this smiling plain,
Where, snake-like coiled, the trenches lie,
In dreams we do not see again
Our bleak hills buttressing the sky.

Think not, within the grim, grey lines,
Haunted by gaunt and grimy men,
Comes no cool chaunting of the pines
That guard one well-remembered glen.

By black hearths in the broken farm,
Bethink ye we remember not
The fire-glow, welcoming and warm,
Which lights the path to one loved cot?—
Bethink ye we remember not?

Here, where the ruined chapels raise
Their blackened beams against the blue,
Comes echo of the hymn of praise
Sung by our home-folk, leal and true.

Here, by the stile, where lovers stood,
And strong hands laboured with the sheaves,

Where are dear drops of human blood
    As crimson as the poppy leaves;

Here, where the ripened harvests rot—
    Where rot an hundred ungraved men,
Bethink ye we remember not
    The little Croft beneath the Ben?
Bethink ye we have aught forgot?
Bethink ye we remember not?

The Tot of Rum

A SOLILOQUY AT STAND-TO IN THE TRENCHES

When the Sergeant drinks your tot, never mind;
When the Sergeant drinks your tot, never mind;
When the sergeant drinks your tot,
Let him drink the bloomin' lot—
Though it burns his bluidy throat
We'll never mind.
SOLDIERS' SONG

Before I saw the trenches
I was a strict T.T.,
The pledge I'd took,
The water brook
Was strong enough for me,
But now I take my tot o' rum—
(I wish to Gawd that Sarg. would come)—
Each morning about three.

It's easy for the blokes at 'ome
To talk of honest water,
And tell us when to take our tot—
(A timble would hold all the lot)—
We really shouldn't oughter;
But if they'd got to stand in mud
And water to the knee,
I guess they'd take their tot o' rum—
(I *wish* to Gawd that Sarg. would come)—
The very same as me.

You've been ten days in the front line,
    Strafed soundly by the Hun,
You're short o' grub, you're short o' sleep,
The water's standing three foot deep,
    You're feeling nearly done;
"Stand-to!" You shiver with the cold
    You've no vitalit-ie—
It's then you bless the tot o' rum—
(I wish to *Gawd* that Sarg. would come,
    It's almost half-past three!)

It's like a warm hand round your heart,
    It's like a brazier's glow;
It trickles through your trembling lips,
It thrills you to your finger-tips,
    And thaws your frozen toe.

"A little for the stomach's sake"—
    That's good enough for me,
To fortify my fainting frame—
I'll give you gospel for the same,
    See Tim. v.23.

When we return from this 'ere war
    To mothers and to wives,
No rum we'll need,
And then we'll lead
    Sober and godly lives.
But while we're fighting in the mud,
    I begs to hope that we
Will get our little tot o' rum—
(My feet is froze, my hands is numb,
Thank Gawd! I see the Sargeant come!)—
    Each morning just at three!

The Mother

"Mother o' mine; O Mother o' mine."

My mother rose from her grave last night,
And bent above my bed,
And laid a warm kiss on my lips,
A cool hand on my head;
And, "Come to me, and come to me,
My bonnie boy," she said.

* * * * *

And when they found him at the dawn,
His brow with blood defiled,
And gently laid him in the earth,
They wondered that he smiled.

Joseph Lee
Flanders '16

Back to London

A Poem Of Leave

I have not wept when I have seen
    My stricken comrades die;
I have not wept when we have made
    The place where they should lie;
My heart seemed drowned in tears, but still
    No tear came to my eye.

There is a time to weep, saith One,
    A season to refrain;
How should it ope, this fount of tears,
    While I sate in the train,
So that all blurred the landscape moved
    Outwith the window pane?

But one short day since I had left
    A land upheaved and rent,
When Spring brings back no bourgeoning,
    As Nature's force were spent;
Yet now I travelled in a train
    Through the kindly land of Kent!

A kindly land, a pleasant land,
    As welcome sight to me
As after purgatorial pains
    The Plains of Heaven might be,
When the wondrous Goodness that is God
    Draws a soul from jeopardy.

A pleasant land, a peaceful land
    Of wooded hill and weald,

Where kine stand knee-deep in the grass
    And sheep graze in the field;
A blessèd land, where a wounded heart
    Might readily be healed.

A wholesome land, where each white road
    Leads to a ruddy hearth;
Where still is heard the sound of song
    And the kindly note of mirth;
Where the strong man cheerful wakes to toil
    And the dead sleep sound i' the earth.

I have not wept when I have seen
    My chosen comrades die;
I have not wept while we have digged
    The grave where they should lie;
But now I lay my head in my hand
    Lest my comrades see me cry.

The little children, two by two,
    Stand on the five-barred gate,
And wave their hands to waft us home
    Like passengers of state;
My heart is very full, so full
    It holds no room for hate.

The children climb the five-barred gate
    And blow us kisses five,
The little cripple in his car
    Waves from the carriage drive:
Blessed are the dead, but blessed e'en more
    We soldiers still alive!

Lo! we draw near to London town,
    The troop train jolts and drags,
The friendly poor come forth once more
    To greet us in their rags—

The very linen on the line
  Flutters and flaunts like flags!

The girls within the factory grim
  Smile at the broken pane;
The sempstress in her lonely room
  Sighs o'er her task again;
The servant shakes her duster forth
  To signal our speeding train;

The station names go flitting past
  Like old familiar friends;
The smoke clouds with the clouds aloft
  In wondrous fashion blends,
And, lo! we enter London town,
  To where all journeying ends.

I have not wept when I have seen
  A hundred comrades die;
I have not wept when that we shaped
  The house where they must lie—
But now I hide my head in my hand
  Lest my comrades see me cry.

These are the scenes, these the dear souls,
  'Mid which our lot was cast,
To this loved land, if Fate be kind,
  We shall return at last,
For this our stern steel line we hold—
  Lord, may we hold it fast!

A BLACK WATCH DINNER IN BELGIUM
MENU
SARDINES ON TOAST
SOUP
SALMON
BEEF
POTATOES
BEANS
HAGGIS
WHISKY
PLUM PUDDING
RICE & FRUIT
COFFEE
CAKE
CIGARETTES
BISCUITS
BON-BONS.
POPERINGHE
4TH JANUARY 1915
7
KANISH
Firmin
Marcel
Pte C A Robb
Mitchell
Maxwell
Cruickshank Sergt
Pipe Major Dan A. McLeod
Johnstone
Octave
Joseph Lee Sgt

Biographies

Caroline Brown is Deputy Archivist at the University of Dundee responsible for the day-to-day management and preservation of the collections. She also has an academic role as Programme Leader for the University's Archives and Family History distance learning programmes. She lectures and publishes on the archive collections and on aspects of archival science and memory and identity. She sits on a number of professional bodies and is on the council of the Scottish Council on Archives.

Matthew Jarron is Curator of Museum Services at the University of Dundee and is the author or editor of several publications including *David Foggie: The Painters' Painter* (2004), *The Artist & the Thinker: John Duncan & Patrick Geddes in Dundee* (2004), *D'Arcy Thompson and his Zoology Museum in Dundee* (2010) and *A Glimpse of a Great Vision: The D'Arcy Thompson Zoology Museum Art Fund Collection* (2014). He has guest edited issues of the *Journal of the Scottish Society for Art History*, *Museum Management & Curatorship* and *Interdisciplinary Science Reviews*, and is currently writing a book on Art in Dundee c.1870-1920. He is currently Chair of the Tayside Museums Forum and General Secretary of the Abertay Historical Society.

Keith Williams is Senior Lecturer in the English at the University of Dundee and chairs the Scottish Word and Image Group. He teaches poetry of the Great War as part of an early twentieth century literature module. His most recent book is *H.G. Wells, Modernity and the Movies* (Liverpool UP, 2007) and he is currently completing a study of *James Joyce and Cinematicity: Before and After Film* for Edinburgh UP.